THE JEWEL

Wolfgang Amadeus Mozart
THE JEWEL BOX
or, *A Mirror Remade*

AN OPERA IN TWO ACTS

———

Libretto by
Carlo Goldoni, Pietro Metastasio, Giuseppe Palomba,
Giuseppe Petrosellini, Lorenzo da Ponte, Giambattista
Varesco, anonymous and *Paul Griffiths*

———

Including songs from the favourite operas of
Lo sposo deluso, Le nozze di Dorina,
Il burbero di buon core, L'astratto, ovvero Il giocatore
fortunato, Le gelosie fortunate, La villanella rapita,
I due baroni di Rocca Azzurra,
L'oca del Cairo, Il curioso indiscreto, etc.

———

Chatto & Windus
LONDON

Published in 1991 by
Chatto & Windus Ltd
20 Vauxhall Bridge Road
London SW1V 2SA

A CIP catalogue record for this work is available
from the British Library

ISBN 0 7011 3862 9

Phototypeset by Intype, London
Printed in Great Britain by
Redwood Press Ltd.,
Melksham, Wiltshire

For John Tyrrell

The Jewel Box was first performed in this translation at the Theatre Royal, Nottingham, on 19 February 1991. The Opera North production was sponsored by Nottinghamshire County Council. The cast was:

DOTTORE	Mark Curtis
PANTALONE	Quentin Hayes
COLOMBINA	Mary Hegarty
PEDROLINO	Barry Banks*
THE COMPOSER	Pamela Helen Stephen
THE SINGER	Jennifer Rhys-Davies
THE FATHER	Stephen Richardson

English Northern Philharmonia
Continuo:	John Querns
Double-bass Obbligato:	Paul Miller
Conductor:	Elgar Howarth
Director:	Francisco Negrin
Designer:	Anthony Baker

*Philip Sheffield sang the part from the pit while Banks, out of voice, acted and spoke the dialogue.

LIST OF CHARACTERS

In order of singing:

DOTTORE, a deceiver	tenor
PANTALONE, a plain man	baritone
COLOMBINA, a heroine	soprano
PEDROLINO, a sad lover	tenor
THE COMPOSER	soprano
THE SINGER, of opera seria	coloratura soprano
THE FATHER	bass

THE ARGUMENT

A comic opera begins ... and ends. The music stops; the characters disintegrate, leaving only archetypes behind them: a deceiver, a plain man, a pair of lovers. How are these outlines to be filled?

The deceiver, Dottore, at first takes charge, and calls on The Composer to carry out his will. But The Composer is immediately more interested in the heroine than in creating a new opera, and is further torn by the interventions in succession of a singer and of someone nearer himself. The first act duly ends in confusion.

Then the plain man, Pantalone, tries to engineer an opera closer to his own desires, though the showing of a deeper level of feeling brings dire consequences to his companions before a solution begins to emerge, with a new opera which is more than Dottore's piece of chicanery or Pantalone's wish-fulfilment.

THE SET

This must be a place where different theatrical worlds can meet. One possibility would be a sequence of curtained proscenium arches, each of which, when opened, reveals another behind. The first, which could be the actual arch of the theatre within which the performance is taking place, might appear for the start of the opening quartet. The second could open for the arrival of The Composer in the ensuing dialogue, the third for The Singer, the fourth for The Father, a fifth for the puppets or automaton, and a sixth for the final new opera.

In the original production the house curtain was lifted at the start of the andante in the overture to show an ultramarine curtain, a section of which was raised to reveal a tiny, tilted set for the quartet. The Composer arrived from the wings, and tore down the ultramarine curtain after Colombina's first aria, discovering behind it a wasteland littered with furniture and a backdrop, and enclosed by a semicircular cyclorama. The Singer eventually emerged behind the backdrop; The Father was revealed behind a portion of the cyclorama; and the miniature theatre for the ending appeared behind another segment.

THE CONTENTS

ACT ONE

ACT TWO

EPILOGUE

NOTE

The Opera North production included all numbers with the exception of No. 14, which was introduced later to provide The Father with a grander exit and to give him a second aria if, as might well be preferred, Nos. 23 and 24 are omitted so that the opera can move directly from the crucial trio (No. 22) to the closing group of numbers.

ACT ONE

No. 1   *Overture*
[D major, allegro-andante, leading into:]

No. 2   *Quartet*   DOTTORE, PANTALONE,
COLOMBINA, PEDROLINO
[D major, allegro]
(According to the stage direction in The Deluded Husband
*the scene is set in a grand ante-chamber giving onto other
rooms. Pantalone is at his toilet, with Dottore standing by.
Colombina and Pedrolino sit at a small table playing cards.)*
DOTTORE
   Ha, ha, ha, ha! It's ridiculous! You as a husband!
PANTALONE
   What's there to laugh about? Right at the start!
   Those darts of love it was, released by Cupid,
   That came to wound me and touch my heart.
DOTTORE
   Pity the girl in this!
   Keep up your courage!
   Lovers of your age
   Rarely persist!
PANTALONE
   Come, let's get on with it! My mind is fixed.
COLOMBINA/PEDROLINO
   Greater stupidity cannot exist.
   No, greater stupidity can't exist.
DOTTORE
   Pity the girl in this!

Watch for the twist!

PANTALONE

Oh but you bore me
With all your scoffing:
You must consider
What's in the offing:
The cynic ends distrusting himself.

COLOMBINA/PEDROLINO

Greater stupidity *etc.*

DOTTORE

Pity the girl *etc.*
Ha, ha, ha, ha *etc.*

PANTALONE

Oh, not all that again . . . Must it restart?
Those darts *etc.*

DOTTORE

Marvellous timepiece! Marvel most marvellous!
And, my, this jewel is most magnificent:
It must be Cartier, it seems to me.

PANTALONE

Gemstone or counterfeit: what does it matter?
(This man who comes here, comes criticising,
Will make me jump up hop, hop, hop, hopping with
    rage!)

DOTTORE

My friend, get ready right away:
Your fiancée's arrived!

PANTALONE

Come, hurry up, get on with it:
I must look in my prime!

PEDROLINO

Signor, I will speak plainly:
You must use more politeness,
More elegance and brightness:
Disorder is a crime.

PANTALONE

Enough of this, to hell with you!
Give me my sword: it's time!

COLOMBINA

If you don't now co-operate,
After our discussions,
There will be repercussions:

PANTALONE

My niece here!

COLOMBINA

Revenge will be sublime!

PANTALONE

My niece here, beginning all her devilment!
Give me my sword: it's time!

DOTTORE

If you don't stop your niece now,
If chaos doesn't cease now,
If you can't make the peace now,
Your bride the stairs will climb!

PANTALONE

So many dreadful nuisances!
Intolerable presences!
I tell you you're excrescences!
Give my my sword: it's time!

QUARTET

(lines 1, 5–8 and 10–18)

(Alarmed by the failure of the music to continue, the four try to repeat the end of the quartet without accompaniment. They dry up. Disconsolately they discard wigs and items of costume that defined them as characters in The Deluded Husband.*)*

Dialogue

DOTTORE

This silence ... This freedom ... We're on our own now.
We're on our own. *(Pause.)* You'll have to do as I say.

Trust me. I'll make it up as we go along. *(Pause. Nothing happens.)*

PANTALONE

Without music . . .

COLOMBINA

. . . what can we feel?

PEDROLINO

What can we do?

PANTALONE

What can we be? *(Pause.)*

DOTTORE

(slowly, but restoring command) Perhaps we need the composer.

(The Composer enters. On his way towards the buffo quartet he finds a large envelope, which he picks up and reads.)

COMPOSER

'To The Composer'. *(He opens it. Inside he finds a red paper heart bearing a message, which he also reads. The details of the message will depend on the production.)* 'Danger. You are about to enter the world of opera buffa. Do not leave the path. Avoid touching the curtain. On no account cross the rail. Do not give your heart away lightly.' *(He laughs.)*

DOTTORE

Ahem. Allow us to introduce ourselves.

COLOMBINA

Colombina, a heroine.

PEDROLINO

Pedrolino, a sad lover.

PANTALONE

Pantalone, a plain man.

DOTTORE

Dottore –

TRIO

(cutting him off) – a deceiver.

4

COMPOSER
> Oh, but don't I know you all by other names? Colombina?
> No ... You're my favourite character! *(He gives her the heart.)*

DOTTORE
> We *have* no characters. The opera ended. That's why we
> need you.

COMPOSER
> I don't see how I can help. 'Colombina', how can I reach
> you?

DOTTORE
> *(to Colombina)* Keep him on the path! Sing one of your
> old songs!

No. 3   *Aria*   COLOMBINA

[G major, andantino grazioso – allegro – andantino grazioso
– allegro – andantino grazioso – allegro]
*(Colombina begins this as a performance, but gradually,
through the repetitions, comes to be meaning it.)*

> You avow that you'll be faithful,
> Like a lover aflame with passion.
> But if marriage were our station,
> Would you falter? Would you alter?
> Tell me: what would your feelings be?
> Would you still be true to me?

> Don't believe it! I can see it!
> You'll be on your way once more.
> Not tonight then, nor tomorrow,
> Will I let you go too far.

Dialogue

COMPOSER
> I will be true! I'll do anything, 'Colombina'! *(He wrenches
> the curtain, or does something else in contravention of the
> red heart's rules.)* What did I do?

DOTTORE
　You broke one of the rules! Your purpose here is simply
　to give us characters!
COMPOSER
　What can I say to her?
DOTTORE
　Not to profess endearments to Colombina!
COMPOSER
　(to Dottore) Why don't you ask her what she feels?
DOTTORE
　(cutting this idea short) The opera, *(pause)* for some reason,
　ended. We need you to make us a new one.
*(The Composer jumps into the set inhabited by the other
four, thus breaking another of the rules and making it poss-
ible, since he is now within the opera, for him to sing.)*

No. 4　　*Aria*　　THE COMPOSER
[C major, andante]
　Can no one, can no one explain it,
　What troubles so my dearest:
　If anger, indecision
　Or fear, suspicion, or love?

　You who know well, O heavens,
　The pureness of my feelings,
　You must resolve this anguish
　Dismaying so my soul!

Dialogue
DOTTORE
　(interrupting) Thank you, but all this is wasting us time.
PANTALONE ·
　And you can't have the girl . . .
PEDROLINO
　. . . because she's mine!

DOTTORE

(hushing them, turning to The Composer) We need an opera from you.

SINGER

(unseen, perhaps amplified) Prence, signor!

COMPOSER

My singer!

DOTTORE

(beginning to be anxious) We need characters!

SINGER

Tutta la Grecia oltraggi tu proteggi il nemico!

COMPOSER

Where is she?

DOTTORE

(insisting) We need something in which to exist!

No. 5   Aria   THE SINGER

[F major, allegro]

(The Singer performs throughout in Italian; an English paraphrase of her words follows the text of the aria. The buffo quartet, terrified at the opening of the orchestral introduction, have gone into hiding before she appears.)

Ah se in ciel, benigne stelle
La pietà non e smarrita,
O toglietemi la vita,
O lasciatemi il mio ben!

Voi, che ardete ognor si belle
Del mio ben nel dolce aspetto,
Proteggete il puro affetto
Che ispirate a questo sen.

[If, o wheel of constellations,
You have space for pity's mending,
Then now grant to me an ending
Or impart to me my love!

You whose bright illuminations
On my lover's face are stealing,
Pray protect my own pure feeling,
Coming likewise from above!]

(Towards the end of the aria The Singer thrusts a book into The Composer's hands. She leaves.)

Dialogue

COMPOSER

(making to leave) I must do what she wants!

DOTTORE

You can't go! Remember why you're here!

PANTALONE

Remember us!

COLOMBINA

Remember me!

PEDROLINO

(threateningly) Remember fear! *(Dottore hushes them again.)*

COMPOSER

Do you really expect me to write you an opera just like that?

DOTTORE

Are you not the composer?

COMPOSER

But I'll need words, a libretto.

DOTTORE

Of course.

COMPOSER

The book! *(He opens it and reads.)* 'The Mirror to Nature, or The Tragic Stage, being a choice of Operatic Libretti, the which include *Olimpiade*', *(others react)* '*L'eroe cinese*', *(others react)* '*Temistocle*', *(others react)* '*Didone abandonnata . . .*' *(others react: the titles are those of the opera seria librettos from which the words of Nos. 5, 9, 14 and*

20 *are taken; 'Temistocle' is omitted if No. 14 is not performed).*

DOTTORE

No more please! Try this book instead!

COMPOSER

(He takes it, opens it, and reads.) 'The Jewel Box, or The Comic Stage, being Some Gems of Operatic Libretti, among them *Luck in Jealousy', (others react) 'The Indiscreet Inquirer', (others react) 'The Fortunate Gambler', (others react) 'The Good-Hearted Grouch . . .'* But it's not so easy. Composing takes time. And then you'd have to learn your parts.

DOTTORE

No problem: we would *be* our parts. Pedrolino, Colombina: positions. Here we bend time to our will. Weeks pass in seconds. Never is now. *(To The Composer, giving him text)* Take this libretto.

COMPOSER

(reading) 'The Village Girl Ravished'.

DOTTORE

If you would be good enough to go back there where you came from, you'll find everything you require. *(The Composer leaves the buffo set. He may find paper, pen, a harpsichord, etc.)* Good. No sooner is the opera written than it comes into being!

(It is as Dottore says: The Composer begins to write and the orchestra starts to play.)

No. 6 **Aria** PEDROLINO
[D major, andante – allegro assai – andante]
(He sings to Colombina, kissing her hand at the end.)
  The goddess of fortune
  Will favour those lovers
  Who prove ever constant
  And burn with desire.

But quickly she counters
Those slow in affection,
Destroying the ventures
Of tentative hearts.

Dialogue

DOTTORE
  Bravo maestro!

COMPOSER
  Thank you, but this wasn't quite what I had in mind.
  Perhaps I should have stayed with that book of
  serious libretti . . .

DOTTORE
  No, no . . .

PEDROLINO
  (to Colombina) I could live with this role.

COLOMBINA
  Could you now?

COMPOSER
  (observing them) What! Another kiss!
  (Pantalone takes him aside.)

No. 7   *Arietta*   PANTALONE
[F major, allegretto]
  A kiss on the fingers
  Is merely a gesture,
  A little imposture:
  They won't go too far.

  It's only an op'ra,
  My dear young composer,
  They may seem improper
  But never ever are.
  Oh no, they never, they never ever are.

In ent'ring the theatre
You must be discreeter:
Impulsive reactions
You really must bar.

A singer's emotions
Are frivolous notions:
Don't take them for real or
Your pleasure you'll mar.

You must close your eyes and
Your ears and your mouth up:
Not seeing or hearing
You'll come to no harm.

It's only an op'ra *etc.*
(*in coda*: They just never are.)

Dialogue

PANTALONE

(*propelling The Composer back to his work*) Back where
you belong! And don't forget: you have to use all of us.

DOTTORE

Eventually, yes. This second scene, however, is simply a
duet.

COMPOSER

Not a love duet!

DOTTORE

Yes, a love duet.

COMPOSER

Very well then, but you may not get quite what you expect ...

No. 8   *Quartet*   PEDROLINO, COLOMBINA,
PANTALONE, DOTTORE
[A major, andante – allegro]

PEDROLINO
Darling, O dearest one, this little gift here:
Take it now, take it now: this is for you.

COLOMBINA
Oh really you are too kind and gracious!
*(At this point The Composer may toss Pedrolino the money,
so perverting the duet.)*
And so much money! From you to me?

PEDROLINO
To you from me.
I'll take your hand in mine
As love's gentle token.

COLOMBINA
Here then, I give it you:
My word unspoken.

COLOMBINA/PEDROLINO
We're so contented,
Can't be resented:
No greater happiness
Could ever be!

PANTALONE
(intervening) Dear composer, carry on there:
Are you sure this is no more than
A professional portrayal,
No ulterior motives hidden?
Nothing hidden, oh sir, no!

PEDROLINO
Colombina, rejoin the others:
I will stay here while you go.

COLOMBINA
Pedrolino means some mischief.
I'm not fooled: I'm sure it's so.

PANTALONE
My suspicions are quite lurid:
I can't help it if you know.

COLOMBINA
He is hazy, slightly crazy:
What you want now I don't know.

DOTTORE
They're returning, and how all this will
Terminate only I know.

Dialogue
*(The Father appears. He carries a jewel box and a mirror.
The buffo quartet again scurry away.)*

PANTALONE
Is this someone else . . .

COLOMBINA
. . . from *her* world . . .

PEDROLINO
. . . the lady with the book . . .?

COMPOSER
The gentleman is my father.

No. 9   Recitative and Aria   THE FATHER
[F major (aria), andante – allegretto – andante]
(He sings to The Composer.)

This is the one I'm seeking! How utterly astounding! His
Features, expression, the voice of this young man, cause
Here within me a curious tremulation. I can't explain it.
However did we get here? The world is in confusion.
I return to a nightmare. My mind is reeling.
I can't even be certain what I am feeling.

Who knows where they come from,
These tender emotions,
This stranger sensation,
That's growing within me,

This chill that I feel
Come gripping my heart?

How could you believe
This was where you were needed?
You have to be gone now
Lest worse should befall.

*(Towards the end of his aria The Father shows The Composer
that the jewel box is empty, the mirror smashed. He motions
The Composer to leave.)*

Dialogue

COMPOSER

I will, Father.

FATHER

Go *now*. This is no place for you.

DOTTORE

He can't go. He's made his choice. Tell him your mind is
changed.

COMPOSER

My mind, sir, is my own.

DOTTORE

Oh no! Not once you stepped off the path! *(or did
whatever he did before No. 4)* Now you belong to *us*.

No. 10   *Aria*   DOTTORE, PANTALONE
[D major, in tempo comodo d'un gran ciarlone ('in a tempo
suiting a great windbag')]

DOTTORE

This young composer must
Be my disciple in
All arts magnetical
And alphabetical,
I shall instruct him in
Matters grammatical,

Studies rhetorical,
Logical, physical
And mathematical:
That cannot fail!

PANTALONE

Hush now, for pity's sake!

DOTTORE

If in his music there
Cannot be unisons,
Tritones or dissonance,
I shall explode!
As for things medical,
Potions and recipes,
Quotients and fractals and
Signs arithmetical,
All the small print in a
Smart lawyer's testament:
All the whole lot soon he
Surely will know!

PANTALONE

Come now, my dear Dottore: you need to be more careful
of this new intruder.

DOTTORE

With charts and measurements,
Nautical compasses,
Then to his heart a com-
Pletely secure way,
Certain and sure way, will
Lie straight ahead.
If you tell me it's an
Impossibility,
I'll test your skeleton's
Inflexibility,
And with one blow I'll split
Your head in two!

PANTALONE

My friend, we should be now continuing the opera. We're
tired of waiting!

DOTTORE

So if you're with me, ap-
Prove my proposal, a
Hundred wild horses I'll
Harness together and
Nottingham, Leeds, also
Birmingham, Manchester,
Sheffield and Hull, York and
Sunderland, Rotherham,
Huddersfield, Doncaster,
Glyndebourne and Darlington
Will guarantee ev'ry-
Thing that I tell to you
Of his great wisdom, in-
Compatability,
Splendour, nobility,
Excellence taught by a
Doctor juridical,
Medical, physical,
Who the whole universe
Will stupefy!

Dialogue

FATHER

(to The Composer) You see how you may be trapped! You
must return!

DOTTORE

(to The Father) You have no power over him! Here he is
ours!

No. 11   **Aria**   THE COMPOSER
[B♭ major, allegro – allegro assai]

(The Composer sings to Dottore, of Colombina.)
  Souls of greatness and noble spirits
  Never pardon indiscretion.
  I am worthy of greater honour,
  And my value is assured.

  Go, deceiver, to that young lady! *(in second section:* deceiver!)
  Tell her this: to her I'm faithful.
  (I'm faithful, I'm faithful, to her ever faithful.)
  But you will not have forgiveness:
  I will now be on my guard!

Dialogue
PANTALONE
  Excuse me if I'm being obtuse, but how does this fit into 'The Village Girl Ravished'?
COMPOSER
  I am not part of the opera! I am not a character! *(He makes to go.)*

No. 12   **Quartet**   COLOMBINA, THE FATHER,
PANTALONE, PEDROLINO
[E♭ major, allegro – allegro assai – più stretto]
COLOMBINA
  So where he goes I will follow!
FATHER
  You can't go: your words are hollow!
COLOMBINA
  You should not have interceded!
PANTALONE
  Are you crazy? You still have to
  Sing the village girl who's ravished, the girl who's ravished.

COLOMBINA
Can't you see that world is finished?
FATHER
(of The Composer) He alone must make the journey.
COLOMBINA
Ah, but those words really burn me!
PANTALONE
But you can't leave Pedrolino.
COLOMBINA
(of The Composer) Here's my darling: Arlecchino.
PANTALONE
Arlecchino? That's not his name!
COLOMBINA
Does it matter? All this chatter
Makes no odds: it's all the same.
FATHER
You must not go –
PANTALONE
If you don't know –
FATHER/PANTALONE
Who he is, this man who's leaving,
And whose song is so deceiving.
COLOMBINA
I believe he is my lover,
And the rest I will discover
When we find our own true home.
You ladies who're blameless,
PANTALONE
You husbands who're flameless,
FATHER
You fathers who're claimless,
TRIO
Who such ills have suffered,
You feel it descending,
This torment unending
That's twisting my heart.

FATHER
You must not go *etc.*

PEDROLINO
Oh stay here, Colombina!

FATHER/PANTALONE
Don't let her go, Pedrolino!

COLOMBINA
(to Pedrolino) You'd not be broken-hearted
If I'd just now departed:
I need to find my own place.

PEDROLINO
But first please tell me why!

COLOMBINA
I feel my life's beginning:
There's something I've been lacking.

PEDROLINO
This wretched composer! Send him packing!

FATHER
Yes, he must go alone.

PANTALONE
We never should have asked him
To help us in our game.

PEDROLINO
(to The Composer) See: you're no longer wanted!
Be off with you, you shadow!

COLOMBINA
Fear makes me tremble so!

FATHER
(of The Composer) If he does not return now
There'll be a great disaster!

PEDROLINO
You nothing! You vapour!
(second time: You figment! You spectre!*)*
(third time: You spirit! You image!*)*

COLOMBINA
O someone stop him!

19

PEDROLINO
   Or now I will make certain . . .
FATHER/PANTALONE
   But don't kill The Composer!
   You'll bring the final curtain!
COLOMBINA
   O heaven! Please stop him!
   Oh please, dear Pedrolino,
   In token of our feelings,
   Forgive, forget, foreswear!
   (repeat last few lines)
QUARTET
   From the way that things are looking
   There can be no compromises.
   We have reached a point of crisis.
   Any more we cannot know.
   With assistance, or else without it,
   We must find somewhere to go.

End of Act One

ACT TWO

Dialogue

DOTTORE

We have to go on . . .

COMPOSER

Perhaps with something from this book *she* gave me . . .
(Dottore goes to interrupt this train of thought; Pantalone intervenes.)

PANTALONE

(shouting) No! *(quietly and deliberately)* No. We'll play it my way now. *(To The Composer)* I don't believe you're really the composer. I think we can get along very well without you. *(The Composer walks away in self-doubt. The Father and Colombina make to go after him. Pantalone calls them back.)* Wait, you two. You can help me get ready.

(The Father is drawn into the ensuing trio against his will: he appeals to The Composer, who is powerless to prevent the number continuing. Colombina is enticed by the prospect Pantalone unfolds. Pedrolino is disconsolate. Dottore is bemused, observing.)

No. 13   *Trio*   PANTALONE, COLOMBINA, THE FATHER

[D major, allegro]

PANTALONE

We need props for this new drama:
Vessels, a table, a statue,
Lances, sword and suits of armour.

Our own staff will soon prepare them:
They'll accept a modest fee.
Sir Dottore, I will tell you
What our roles will have to be.
Then of shirts we'll need a hundred,
Pairs of shoes and hose unnumbered.
Order wigs to come from London:
We'll be wanting thirty-three.
Have no fear about the décor:
You can leave that up to me.

COLOMBINA

What about the hats and dresses?

PANTALONE

You will wear them soon, my guess is.

FATHER

Jewel boxes, looking glasses?

PANTALONE

Will be worthy of a lord.
We shall have the very finest:
Better than you'd find abroad!
(to Colombina) To you I give charge of
The stables, the wardrobe,
The dressers, the grooms and
The rest of that horde.
(to The Father) You go and get ready
The pantry, the kitchen,
The plates, food and drink:
All the best we'll afford!
And when I command it
We'll have our first chord.

COLOMBINA

I'm willing, sir, and able:
A young girl in a stable
Is very rarely bored.

FATHER

Your orders, sir, are nice, sir:

I'll make a coffee ice, sir.
(This whole thing's untoward!)
PANTALONE
Go on now, make ready,
Be off now, but listen:
You must all be careful
And work in accord!
repeat from To you I give charge of
PANTALONE
This greatest occasion
Imposes elation:
Join hands to applaud!
TRIO
tercets I'm willing, Your orders *and* This greatest . . .

Dialogue
PANTALONE
Thank you, Colombina, and – (*He turns to The Father,
who breaks away.*)

No. 14   Recitative and Aria   THE FATHER
[F minor (aria), allegro]
(*He sings to The Composer.*)

You see we don't belong here! We must go now together!
Such folly! So come now: come with your dearest father!
(*The Composer silently indicates that he intends to remain
with Colombina.*)
You want to stay with her, want to remain here . . . That
cannot happen! No! We must leave here: come now! Come
back now, back now! In your past is your future: there's
no escaping what reality offers. Beyond the threshold you
have erred into danger, into utter confusion.
(*The Composer refuses The Father's invitation to leave.*)
Then you will stay within this world of delusion!

This is a bitter lesson,
Child of my deep devotion!

You must now feel the emotion
That thunders in my heart!

I beg you now to listen:
There can be no (more) delaying.
You know that we're not playing:
You have no other part!

(He leaves.)

Dialogue
*(If No. 14 is omitted, the dialogue proceeds as follows
directly after No. 13. If No. 14 is used, the dialogue picks
up again with Dottore's words below.)*

FATHER

   (to The Composer) You see what they're making of us?
   We don't belong in this world. Come now.

COMPOSER

   I have to stay. I have to stay with her *(i.e. Colombina)*.

FATHER

   Then I leave you to your fate! *(He leaves.)*

DOTTORE

   Pay no attention! We still have everybody we need for the
   new opera, if The Composer would return to his work and
   Colombina to Pedrolino –

PANTALONE

   We don't need this composer! *(He moves in to seize Colombina for himself.)*

No. 15   *Aria*   PANTALONE
[D major, allegro – allegro molto]
   Take a look at Pantalone
   And you'll see the state of play.
   Hear me saying: I'm freezing, I'm burning,
   O my love, give way, give way!

Yes, my darling, just a moment:
Turn your eyes towards your lover,
And in mine you will discover
What my lips could never say.

A Guglielmo in lovesick fashion
Cannot match me in my ardour.
A Ferrando, protesting passion,
Next to me must try much harder.

This is fire I am exhaling;
My desire remains unfailing.
If my value you are doubting,
Hear me tell you, no: hear me shouting,
That you cannot find my equal
Right from here to Hudson's Bay!

I am quite as rich as Croesus,
And in beauty like Narcissus,
While the heat of my adoring
Makes Mark Antony look boring.
Bars of iron I can break shear;
I can write (too) as well as Shakespeare.

When I'm dancing, inspect my shin: see
I'm as nimble as Nijinsky.
When I sing, with trill so comely,
All the songbirds just sit there dumbly.
And I have still other merits
That I'll tell another day.
(Colombina goes to The Composer. Pantalone breaks down.)

Wonder, wonder: she won't waver.
Aren't you pleased at her behaviour?
Her devotion's ever constant;
You're the one she won't betray!

No. *16*   *Gigue*   HARPSICHORD SOLO
(There is some scenic demonstration of the artificiality of this world. In the original production the buffo quartet walked slowly towards a false harpsichord at the front of the stage, and then behind them four marionettes of themselves dropped down. They turned. Pedrolino went forward to take his puppet in his hands. Another possibility might be the arrival of an automaton seeming to play, or indeed actually playing, the gigue. For the buffo quartet, though, this is not a comic moment, and the audience should not be prevented from feeling that.)
COMPOSER
   You see? This is all you are!

No. *17*   *Rondò*   PEDROLINO
[Eb major, andante – allegro assai – adagio – allegro assai]
   Please don't ask, in all compassion,
   Why you see me here tormented.
   So intense is my dejection
   Even I cannot adjust!

   I consider . . . But how can I . . .?
   An escape . . . But can I really
   Hope for any resolution
   When there's nothing I can trust?

   Ah, in rage and indignation
   That my hopes cannot be mended,
   Hear me wish my life were ended:
   Death is now my only prayer!

(He kills himself with a dagger.)

Dialogue
DOTTORE
   (to Pantalone, with bitter irony) Is this what you intended?

PANTALONE
   (quietly) No . . .
COMPOSER
   (with some anxiety) You're all just shadows!

No. *18*   *Aria*   THE SINGER
[C major, allegro – allegro assai]
(She enters and suddenly sings to The Composer.)
   No, che non sei capace
   Di cortesia, d'onore,
   E vanti a torto un core
   Ch'arde d'amore per me.
(She indicates a door or curtain through which The Composer must go.)
   Vanne! T'abhorro, ingrato,
   E piu me stesso abhorro,
   Che t'ho un istante amato,
   Che sospirai per te.

   [No, you still have not within you
   Any sense of shame or kindness,
   And in such a state of blindness
   You can feel no love for me.

   Go! I hate your constant coldness,
   And yet more I turn that hatred
   On myself, who had the boldness
   Once to think your love I'd be.]

(She leaves.)

No. *19*   *Aria*   THE COMPOSER
[E♭ major, allegro – andante sostenuto]
   Onward! But where now? O heaven!
   What are you asking from me?
   Where can I find the answer?

How can I understand?
(How can I find out the truth?)

Love, you I know will guide me,
Stay on my way beside me.
Take from me these misgivings,
Unloose my heart from doubt.

(He leaves through the door or curtain shown by The Singer.)

No. 20   *Recitative and Aria*   COLOMBINA

[E♭ major (aria), andantino espressivo – allegretto – andante espressivo]

(She is distraught at the disappearance of The Composer, and remembers too her love for Pedrolino. Towards the end of the aria she finds his dagger.)

Enough. It's over. I can go no further. You knew how I
adored you, despite rejection. The first time that our eyes
   met
You saw my feelings waver, my look deceive me.
And yet now you betray me, can dare to leave me?

Ah, do not leave me, no,
My dear beloved.
In whom can I believe
If not my lover?

One word alone will kill me,
If we must say farewell (now).
From such a pain as fills me
No soul could recover.

(She kills herself.)

Dialogue

DOTTORE

> *(to Pantalone)* You see how well your little scheme is turning out for you! My congratulations!

No. 21   *Aria*   DOTTORE

[C major, allegro assai]

(Mockingly he gathers up the dagger and whatever other props are lying about, and delivers them to Pantalone.)

> With due rev'rence, and respect, sir,
> I bow down, sir, and then kow-tow, sir,
> To a man of such great wisdom
> That the world contains no equal,
> That no equal could exist
> (For outrageous pride and dumbness
> And complete stupidity)!

No. 22   *Trio*   PANTALONE, PEDROLINO,

COLOMBINA

[E♭ major, andantino]

PANTALONE

> Such reverses! Such a drama!
> I am speechless. What to do?

PEDROLINO

> I'm bewildered. I'm dumbfounded.

(Pantalone is astonished that the apparently dead Pedrolino should suddenly sing: astonished and then delighted.)

> And I don't know what is true.

PANTALONE

> It may be I'm really dreaming
> And will wake to what I knew . . .

COLOMBINA

> So I'm living, and death is over?

(Again astonishment and delight, from Pedrolino as well as Pantalone.)

PEDROLINO

Ah my love, what can I hope for?

PANTALONE

You revive and so does she!

COLOMBINA/PEDROLINO

Great alarm I feel within me:

My heart starts to palpitate.

PANTALONE

My heart slips a beat within me:

I do not exaggerate!

I am speechless.

PEDROLINO

I'm bewildered.

COLOMBINA

I'm dumbfounded.

TRIO

Strange awak'ning! Someone tell us

What we now must do together. What now?

I begin to feel myself reborn.

We are changing all at once!

PEDROLINO

Strange new world!

PANTALONE

Someone tell us –

COLOMBINA

Strange new world!

TRIO

Someone tell us *etc.*

(*The three begin to find new costumes under their old ones, though their emergent personae are not yet evident.*)

Dialogue

(*The harpsichord prepares for D major.*)

PANTALONE

Ah! Is this where we get some recitative at last?

COLOMBINA
I think we've left all that behind, don't you?

No. 23   Andante
[D major (reprise from No. 1)]
(The Composer and The Father return together. They bring with them the remaining costume necessities and also a jewel box covered in mirror. Inside this will be a flute and a bird, though nothing is yet revealed, nor is it yet clear that The Father too has been transformed.)

No. 24   Aria   THE FATHER
[D major, andante – allegro – adagio – allegro]

(He sings to The Composer on behalf of the others. The double-bass soloist is on a podium in the pit.)

By what this hand's creating,
By what these eyes engender,
I'll be your first defender:
We swear our love for you.

Rivers and flowers and forests,
That witnessed my complaining,
Will tell you I'm not feigning
A love that's sure and true.

Give me kind(ly) or haughty glances,
Tell me that you hate or love me,
In my heart your music dances,
In my mind you sing above me.
Neither flood nor fire can alter
The respect that is your due.

Dialogue

PEDROLINO

(pointing to what The Composer and The Father have brought.)

Is this everything we still need?

COMPOSER

Yes: now we can all be what we must.

FATHER

Now we can get ready to go.

COLOMBINA

Just a moment . . .

(Just a moment indeed, because other events here are possible. No. 24 may be omitted, in which case the above dialogue follows No. 23 directly. Or No. 23 may be omitted, in which case No. 24 follows the dialogue after No. 22 directly, and The Composer and The Father make their return during the introduction to the aria. Or both No. 23 and No. 24 may be omitted, in which case No. 25 follows No. 22 directly, without harpsichord or dialogue, and The Composer, The Father and The Singer all come on – perhaps together, perhaps from different places – during the introduction to that aria. In this last case the opera proceeds entirely without speech from No. 21 to the end.)

No. 25   *Aria*   THE SINGER
[A major, adagio – allegro – più allegro]
(She sings to The Composer.)

Vorrei spiegarvi, oh Dio!
Qual è l'affanno mio;
Ma mi condanna il fato
A piangere e tacer.

Arder non può il mio core
Per chi vorrebbe amore
E fa che cruda io sembri,
Un barbaro dover.

Amico, partite,
Correte, fuggite
Lontano da me.
Il vostro diletto
Teatro v'aspetta,
Languir non lo fate,
È degno d'amor.

Ah stelle spietate!
Nemiche mi siete.
Mi perdo s'ei resta, Oh Dio!
Partite, correte,
D'amor non parlate,
Loro il vostro cor.

[They need, o God, expression,
Such feelings – a confession –
But fate is now my master:
I must say nought and weep.

My love here stands forbidden;
Through strength it can be hidden:
To him I must seem cruel;
The anguish I can keep.

My friend, you must leave me:
Go, hurry, believe me:
Your journey is long.
You now will discover
The theatre's your lover.
It will not receive me:
It waits for your song.

O stars, how you grieve me,
That once did deceive me!
I must still be strong!

Depart now and leave me;
Love cannot reprieve me:
Go where you belong!]

(The Composer goes out into a miniature theatre revealed at the rear. He might take his place in the auditorium.)

No. 26   German Dance
[D major]
(The lights go up to reveal that Pantalone, Pedrolino, Colombina and The Father have completed their transformation into Papageno, Tamino, Pamina and Sarastro. This could be clinched by the first two finding the bird and the flute within the mirrored jewel box. They prepare to leave into the theatre beyond, where the stage might be set for The Magic Flute. *Pamina could encourage The Singer to go with them: she is now The Queen of the Night. Dottore could be left alone, Pamina kissing him farewell, or else he could be given a mask to appear as the monster at the start of the new opera. In the original production Pantalone, Pedrolino, Colombina and The Father followed The Composer out into the miniature theatre and away, leaving Dottore by himself in the old set.)*

End of Act Two

EPILOGUE

No. 27   *Aria*   THE COMPOSER
[G major, andante]
(He quietens the applause to sing on behalf of the cast.)
   Now take our thanks, you gentle patrons:
   You bring such warmth into our hearts!
   Were I a man, I'd speak it clearly,
   But as I am I've not the art.

   Yet know, until our final moments,
   We won't forget you or your grace!
   If we could stay we would endeavour
   To really earn it, but enough.

   In ev'ry time the lot of artists
   Has been to move from place to place.
   We're no exception to this ruling:
   We have to leave you now to go

   And follow where our fate may lead us.
   Yet know, wherever we may be,
   Throughout the world of space and time,
   We will be here: our hearts with you.

End of opera

AFTERNOTE

The Jewel Box is most essentially a case of effect (music) preceding cause (words); perhaps for that reason a certain amount of chronological doubt hangs about it, in that it is impossible to be sure whether a particular phrase or idea in the libretto was sparked off by something in Mozart's life or works, or whether it found confirmation there. For example, I thought of using the commedia dell'arte at an early stage (not such a great claim to make when the old masks are so close behind the faces of standard opera buffa characters, and when they have gained a new operatic life this century in, for instance, *Ariadne auf Naxos*, *Arlecchino* and *The Love for Three Oranges*) and only later came across Mozart's letter of 12 March 1783 in which he tells his father about a pantomime, given with his own music by a company including himself as Harlequin, Aloysia Lange as Columbine, Joseph Lange as Pierrot, a painter as the Doctor and 'an old dancing master' as Pantaloon. Here all at once were the figures for the opening quartet, together with The Composer who might just possibly be Harlequin in disguise. Here, too, was the hint of a doubleness in the presentation of Aloysia Lange, who already had to be on stage in another form as the singer of the flamboyant coloratura music Mozart wrote for her: she could now be here both as a person among friends (Colombina) and as an artist on display (The Singer), or both as Mozart's desired image and as the distant reality, or both as his love object and as an inspiring virtuoso. However, it is perfectly possible that a memory of the Mozart letter was in my mind all along. And his final comment on

37

the subject seemed to be a warning against understanding words as locked into a particular occasion: 'The verses . . . might have been done better. I had nothing to do with them.'

But his disclaimer, at least where *The Jewel Box* is concerned, goes too far, since although he had been dead for very nearly two centuries before the piece reached the stage, my effort was to allow decisions about the libretto to arise as far as possible from the music. The whole purpose, after all, was to restore this music to the theatre, for which it was conceived: *The Jewel Box* was to be, simply in its existence, a demonstration that the composer's role in opera is paramount. It would have been absurd to rescue all these pieces and then imprison them again in a libretto derived from outside, whether a genuine eighteenth-century text (I briefly toyed with the idea of using one of those Lorenzo da Ponte had written for other composers), a pastiche, or something new. The libretto would have to come out of the given arias and ensembles: these would have to be words listening to music.

For reasons already touched on, it is the history of the music that is easier to relate. In Mozart's time no opera had a stable existence outside the conditions of performance. Mozart himself made alterations to all the operas of his that had notable revivals during his lifetime (*La finta giardiniera, Idomeneo, The Marriage of Figaro* and *Don Giovanni*); had he lived longer we might well be confronted with a greater abundance of rival texts. He also wrote arias and ensembles to be inserted into the works of other composers: eleven arias and two ensembles, counting only those written for Italian comedies.

The first batch of comic insert arias date from 1775 and 1776, when he was nineteen and twenty, and living in Salzburg; they thus come soon after *La finta giardiniera*, which had its first performance in Munich in January 1775.

There was then a gap of three years in his operatic output,

before the unfinished *Zaide* (1779–80). During that time he went on a long journey alone, staying in Mannheim during the winter of 1777–8 and in Paris for the following spring and summer. While in Mannheim he evidently fell in love with Aloysia Lange, and rashly wrote to his father that he would travel penniless to Italy in order to write operas for her: his father responded firmly that he should make some money in Paris first. Then in 1781 he decisively left his family home and his Salzburg appointment to settle in Vienna. *Idomeneo* had been presented, again in Munich, at the start of that year; *The Abduction from the Seraglio* followed in Vienna in 1782.

The next year the court theatre reverted to opera in Italian, and Mozart wrote three insert arias for Anfossi's *The Indiscreet Inquirer*, to be sung by Aloysia Lange and by Valentin Adamberger. Probably also in that year he began two abortive Italian comedies of his own, *The Deluded Husband* and *The Cairo Goose*. After that came another gap before the autumn of 1785, when he began *The Marriage of Figaro* and also wrote two ensembles for a Vienna performance of Bianchi's *The Village Girl Ravished*. *Don Giovanni* followed in 1787, and then in 1788 its Vienna revival, after which Francesco Albertarelli, who had sung the title role, was rewarded with an aria for his part in another Anfossi opera. The final group of three insert arias was composed the next year for Louise Villeneuve, shortly to create the role of Dorabella in *Così fan tutte*.

So here was a total of thirteen numbers, to which could be added three more ensembles and an overture completed for the two unfinished operas – and there was good reason to add ensembles when, as has often been remarked, one of the distinguishing features of Mozart's comedies is their density of ensembles (it would also be useful to have an overture). Attempts have been made, and continue to be made, to complete *The Deluded Husband* and *The Cairo Goose*, but in both cases one has to add extraneous material and finish numbers which Mozart only sketched. As for the arias and ensembles written as insertions, they could only be presented in their original contexts by staging a whole opera by some other composer for the sake of a few minutes of Mozart, and in some cases there is no certain record of the opera for which an aria was composed. Also, many of these pieces are not suitable as concert items. The arias Mozart wrote specifically for concert performance are substantial movements, nearly always with an opening recitative in which the singer can both warm up and establish a reason for singing. Most of the insert arias are shorter, and begin without musical and dramatic justification, which would have come from the original opera. The ensembles are even unlikelier concert repertory, and lack the life which some of the arias have gained in recorded recitals; beside which, this is all music written to be heard from the stage.

Hence *The Jewel Box*. There is a strong eighteenth-century precedent for assembling diverse arias into a new whole: the tradition of the *pasticcio*, defined in *The New Grove* as 'a dramatic or sacred vocal work whose parts have been wholly or partly borrowed from existing works by various composers'. The same dictionary goes on to quote words from the *argomento* of Boldini's *L'abbandono d'Armida* (Venice, 1729), words which the librettist of *The Jewel Box* can only echo in saying that his aim has been to 'combine in a certain scenic harmony and in an appropriate order those arias which were created and performed at other times, in other places and under different conditions, and which have been reintroduced with the sole purpose of renewing the pleasure which is to be had from them.' The pleasure to be renewed was that of Mozart's music: I therefore immediately discounted the idea of newly composed recitative. This would have to be an opera with spoken dialogue, and since I would be writing the dialogue in English, the musical numbers too would be given in translation.

The first tasks – and now we have re-entered the cloudy

history of the libretto – were to arrange the seventeen numbers in an order and to define the characters who would sing them. The two decisions were, of course, interwoven, since one of the constraints had to be that the singers' loads had to be spread: that one could not ask someone to sing two strenuous arias (and most of these are indeed strenuous arias: Mozart was not bashful to shine in his insertions) in succession, and that each singer should have the chance to make a mark in each of the two acts (and it seemed a sensible accommodation to modern theatre practice to make this a two-act opera). The ensembles, too, would have to be well spaced, in the interests of variety. In order to cut down further the choices of order, and also to give this inevitably diverse piece some musical continuity, I decided that the opera would have to end back in the key of the overture, D major, and that shifts of tonality would have to be, as in *The Marriage of Figaro*, by thirds and fifths. All these limitations very usefully reduced the options, but they also suggested more numbers would be needed, either to give singers a suitable number of arias or to cover gaps in the key scheme.

The cast of seven had quickly established themselves from inspection of the ensembles. The opening quartet of *The Deluded Husband* is for a soprano, two tenors and a baritone, while the quartet for *The Village Girl Ravished* requires soprano, tenor, baritone and bass voices. That indicated a minimum of five singers, but since six of the arias are for soprano, there clearly had to be more than one voice of that type; and indeed the two arias for Lange are very distinct in style and, most particularly, register from the other two. It also seemed a good idea, in an opera in need of any trace of coherence it could find, to create one character as singing only Louise Villeneuve music. Similarly, the four tenor arias at once suggested two different voices, of lyric and character types. So there would be seven singers: a coloratura soprano (singing Lange's music), a high mezzo (singing Villeneuve's), another soprano, a lyric tenor, a character tenor, a baritone and a bass. Nos. 9, 26 and (later) 14 were introduced to make good the total deficiency of bass arias; No. 20 was added to give 'another soprano' (eventually Colombina) a second aria; and No. 15 – which Mozart removed from *Così fan tutte* before the first performance, and which therefore has no rightful place there – was subsequently added to the baritone part.

As for what these voices should represent, it seemed to me that the necessary openness and malleability of the drama would best be achieved if the characters could come from different levels of operatic reality. One of them obviously had to be the composer, whom I initally named as Mozart. Mozart could not possibly be a bass, nor could he be any of the other men, because they were all involved in the opening comic quartet. Nor, most particularly, could he be a coloratura soprano. The Villeneuve music, however, seemed exactly right in its youthful ardour and its high musical sophistication, all of it coming from the period of *Così*. The Lange music could then be sung by an embodiment of Lange herself, representing the race of singers, and I added a third Lange aria to the two from *The Indiscreet Inquirer*. It was part of my original intention that this character should perform consistently in Italian, in her arias and in her dialogue, since it would have been hard to find English words to fit her elaborate vocal spinning, such words would have been an extra handicap to the singer, and they would not have been understood anyway. I also thought the performer of this role deserved the side-benefit of being able to add the arias to her concert repertory (and I was delighted to learn later from Jennifer Rhys-Davies, who created the Lange role in *The Jewel Box*, that she had not sung any of her music before). But of course there would have to be some dramatic reason why this Italian singer was bursting into an English-language opera, a reason I at first found in envisaging the Aloysia Lange of the piece as believing herself to be Elettra in a performance of *Idomeneo*: all her spoken lines would be quotations from Elettra's recitatives (as indeed the two that remain in the present text are), and she would imagine the others on stage to be part of the same opera gone terrifyingly awry: Mozart as Idamante, the other soprano as Ilia, and so on. Meanwhile this other soprano would think herself to be a character, Susanna, who would take Mozart to be Cherubino; or perhaps she was Constanze leading him a dance. The two tenors would be wholly absorbed in themselves as voices, First Tenor and The Other First Tenor, arguing about their relative priority in the manner of the sopranos of *The Impresario*. The baritone would be an archetype, Pantalone; and the bass would be a real person, singing under his own name and remaining aloof from the others' games, like a Sarastro or a Don Alfonso. The piece would begin with him and Mozart seated outside the main action.

That was the point the opera, still untitled, had reached by the summer of 1988, when the idea that 1991 would be Mozart Year was still unrecognised by anyone but record company executives, and when I was making an annual visit to the Opera Theatre of Saint Louis on behalf of *The Times*. I mentioned the idea to people there, and was encouraged to go ahead and write the libretto, which I got around to doing in the early months of 1989. The Saint Louis company were not immediately overwhelmed, and I put the thing aside, glad at least to have been brought close to the music and made to think a little about how to make an opera.

Then in the summer of 1989 Opera North presented *La finta giardiniera*, in an English version by Amanda Holden, but with a note in the programme by the company's general administrator, Nicholas Payne, pointing out that there were just three words in the piece that had eluded translation: those of the title. I filled a couple of postcards with more or less silly suggestions ('She Stoops to Compost'), and had back from Payne a postcard from Salzburg, in which he said he was looking for some unusual Mozart to do in 1991, so far without success. Of course I responded by proposing *The*

Jewel Box, which I rewrote, and which he accepted in December.

After that we waited. I had always considered the libretto merely a draft that would have to be reworked in the light of consultations with a director, but no director could be found willing to risk his or her reputation on the venture until September 1990, when Francisco Negrin entered the story. By this time the opera already had a cast, a conductor, and a date for the first performance, with previews in January 1991. All it lacked was a final libretto and a production.

In the middle of October I spent a day talking with Negrin, who had two principal problems with my sketch: he wanted the musical numbers more deeply embedded in the drama, not delivered as recitations; and he wanted everyone on stage all the time. That first requirement meant compressing the levels of the original version somewhat, so that 'Susanna' and the two tenors joined Pantalone as commedia archetypes, and the bass came nearer the dimension of Mozart and Aloysia: giving these three generic names avoided a metaphor being taken as a biography, and also made explicit the homage to The Composer of a later composer, Richard Strauss. The desire for a more consistent dramatic world also gave me permission to alter the sung texts, which I had avoided doing: in particular, the words of Nos. 7, 8, 9, 12, 13, 14 and 22 depart considerably from what Mozart set. The second stipulation had interesting consequences, too. My original libretto had been a sequence of short scenes involving two, three or four characters, with a great number of exits and entrances, the exits necessitated, as I thought, by the nature of the music. How, for instance, could someone sing No. 17, with its repeated passionate assertions 'Death is now my only prayer!', and then remain on stage? The only possible solution, in this case and in that of No. 20, was suicide, with No. 22 neatly making it possible for the two victims to come to life again. Miraculously, even a justification for this arrived the next year when I read in Daniel Heartz's *Mozart's Operas*

(University of California Press, 1990), *à propos* the 1783 pantomime, that 'it may be presumed, on the basis of *commedia dell'arte* traditions, that Harlequin comes back to life, after having been killed'. Mozart would not, after all, have found *The Jewel Box* so strange.

The piece went into rehearsal in late November 1990, and was subsequently altered again, before and after the previews given in Leeds in the second week of January 1991. The text published here was fashioned on, and in some cases by, the singers concerned; it also owes debts to the director, conductor and designer of the first production. But the finale was always a problem. In my first version I had simply had the unnamed bass announce to the assembled company that what they had been looking for was an exit in the necessary key of D major, provided by the extraordinary German Dance that fitted this piece so well: there was no grand septet among Mozart's operatic leavings, and so only a dance could involve everyone, and only this particular dance could do so with wildness and an ironic shrug. But in the new version something was beginning to happen in the second act: the trio (No. 22) was taking them on somewhere. But where?

There was not, it seemed to me, the musical support for an enlightenment such as is achieved, however uncertainly, in the endings of *Figaro* or *Così fan tutte*. Nor could this crucial moment be clinched in the text: that would have been to assume an excessive degree of authority over the music – something I had been avoiding. Only after the first preview did I hit on a solution, the solution contained here, by which time, of course, the set and costumes had long been determined. I must, therefore, reiterate thanks to all those involved in the Opera North production, who have, sometimes against their wills, gone along with this attempt to activate whatever will could be discovered in some unsuspecting music.

Paul Griffiths

APPENDIX: A LITTLE JEWEL BOX
ENCYCLOPAEDIA

Abstracted Man, The *(L'astratto, ovvero Il giocatore fortunato)* Opera by Piccinni to a libretto by Petrosellini. Mozart wrote two arias for the same much reworked scene, but on different occasions, 'Con ossequio' (No. 21) being dated May 1775 and 'Clarice cara' (No. 10) September 1776. The latter comes first in the action. Capitano Faccenda, disguised as the learned Dottore Testa Secca, ridiculously courts Clarice, the daughter of Don Timoteo, distracting attention while his sister makes off with Don Timoteo's son; Don Timoteo keeps trying to interrupt. Then Don Timoteo angrily pays mock homage to the presumed doctor, though this must be in a different production, since Don Timoteo is now a tenor whereas he was a baritone in the other aria.

Adamberger, Valentin (1743–1804) German tenor. He sang in Vienna from 1780 until his retirement in 1793, and created the role of Belmonte, besides singing in the first performance of several other Mozart works. 'Per pietà' (No. 17) was written for him to sing in *The Indiscreet Inquirer*, though he was dissuaded – according to Mozart, through a scheme of Salieri's – from using it.

Albertarelli, Francesco Italian bass. He sang in Vienna from 1788 to 1790, and later in London. In May 1788 he was Don Giovanni in the first Viennese performance of the opera, and that same month Mozart wrote 'Un bacio di mano' (No. 7) for him to sing in *The Lucky Jealous Women*.

Anfossi, Pasquale (1727–97) Italian composer. Possibly a pupil of Piccinni, he worked mostly in Rome and Venice, though with a spell in London in the 1780s. Of his numerous operas, both serious and comic, Mozart wrote insert arias for two: *The Indiscreet Inquirer* and *The Lucky Jealous Women*.

Benucci, Francesco (*c.* 1745–1824) Italian bass. He first sang in Vienna in 1783: Mozart, eager to write an opera buffa at the time, heard the company and found him 'particularly good'. He was based largely in Vienna then until 1795, and appeared there as Figaro, Leporello and Guglielmo; he was also the intended Bocconio in *The Deluded Husband*, and so Nos. 2, 15 and 22 were all written with him in mind.

Bianchi, Francesco (1752–1810) Italian composer. He wrote a great many operas for various Italian cities and also for London, where he lived from 1794 until his suicide. Mozart wrote two ensembles for his *The Village Girl Ravished*.

Bussani, Francesco (1743–after 1807) Italian bass. He sang in Vienna from 1783 to 1794, his roles including Doctor Bartolo and Antonio, the Commendatore and Masetto, and Don Alfonso, as well as Biagio in *The Village Girl Ravished*.

Cairo Goose, The (*L'oca del Cairo*) Unfinished opera by Mozart to a libretto by Varesco. In May 1783 Mozart asked his father to find out if Varesco could write him 'a new libretto for seven characters': as in *The Jewel Box*, there were to be three women ('one of these to be seria') and four men. Varesco duly supplied a libretto in which the hero disguises himself inside a wooden goose in order to visit his beloved, whom her father keeps confined in a tower. Mozart drafted arias, ensembles and a finale for the first of the three acts, but despaired of the libretto and seems to have abandoned the thing by February 1784. One number (No. 13), however, exists in a complete form, possibly finished and orchestrated by Johannes Simon Mayr. Here Don Pippo is looking forward to his intended marriage, and instructs his servants Auretta and Chichibio to make preparations.

Calvesi, Vincenzo Italian tenor. He was the leading Italian lyric tenor in Vienna for most of the time from 1785 to 1794, his roles including Ferrando and the Count in *The Village Girl Ravished*.

Cavalieri, Catarina (1760–1801) Viennese soprano. She made her debut in 1775 and later became Salieri's mistress. Her Mozart roles included Constanze, Donna Elvira and the Countess, and the part of Bettina in *The Deluded Husband* was meant for her.

Chinese Hero, The *(L'eroe cinese)* Libretto by Metastasio. Mozart chose from it the text for 'Ah se in ciel' (No. 5), written for Aloysia Lange and dated 4 March 1788 in his catalogue, though a version of the piece was composed a decade earlier. The words belong to the Tartar princess Lisinga, who is the prisoner of the Chinese regent and in love with his son Siveno. Her father has told her she must marry the Chinese heir, but since the entire imperial family has been wiped out in a revolt, she and Siveno are filled with dread about who the heir might be and about their impending separation.

Cimarosa, Domenico (1749–1801) Italian composer. His operas, especially the comedies, were in international demand. Mozart died just two months before his most successful work, *The Clandestine Marriage*, had its first performance in Vienna. The insert aria 'Alma grande' (No. 11) was written for another widely disseminated piece, *The Two Barons of Rocca Azzurra*.

Colombina The spirited low-born heroine of the commedia dell'arte.

Coltellini, Celeste (1760–1829) Italian soprano. She sang in Vienna in 1785, notably in the title role of *The Village Girl Ravished*. Later she created the title role in Paisiello's *Nina*.

Così fan tutte Opera by Mozart to a libretto by da Ponte. The Guglielmo aria 'Rivolgete a lui' (No. 15) was replaced before the first performance and listed separately by Mozart in his catalogue under December 1789.

Deluded Husband, The *(Lo sposo deluso, ovvero La rivalità di tre donne per un solo amante)* Unfinished opera by Mozart.

There is no certain reference to this work in Mozart's letters, though in July 1783 he mentioned that 'an Italian poet' had brought him a libretto, 'which I shall perhaps adopt, if he agrees to trim and adjust it in accordance with my wishes'. If this was *Lo sposo deluso*, the libretto was one that Cimarosa had set in 1780 as *Le donne rivali*, and the original text may have been by Petrosellini: Mozart here was following his practice in *La finta giardiniera*, when he had re-set a libretto, also probably by Petrosellini, written for Anfossi. Mozart's copy of the libretto for *The Deluded Husband* indicates that the cast was to have included Cavalieri, Storace and Benucci.

The music Mozart drafted comprises the overture and four numbers, all from the first half of the first act: the trio (No. 22) is finished, and the overture and quartet (Nos. 1–2) nearly so, the wind parts, where secondary, having been filled in by another hand, presumably for the concert Constanze Mozart gave in Prague in 1797; the two arias are complete as vocal lines with bass and a few details of the first violin part only. In the quartet Bocconio, the deluded husband of the title, is preparing himself to meet his bride Eugenia and is beset by his misogynist friend Pulcherio, by his vain niece Bettina, and by Don Asdrubale, an officer who is in love with Eugenia but loved by Bettina. Eugenia duly arrives, but only after Don Asdrubale has left: the trio of astonishment comes later, when they meet. She had thought him dead in battle; he had thought her to be in Rome; Bocconio realises that something is going on.

Dido Abandoned *(Didone abandonnata)* Libretto by Metastasio. Mozart drew Dido's plea from it for 'Basta! Vincesti' (No. 20), written for Dorothea Wendling in Mannheim, and dated 27 February 1778.

Dottore The charlatan scholar of the commedia dell'arte, pretending to knowledge and wisdom he lacks, and gulling the others (and himself, though not the audience).

Fischer, Ludwig (1745–1825) German bass. He sang in

Vienna in 1780–3, during which time he was the first Osmin. Later Mozart wrote No. 9 for him, and possibly also No. 14.

Galuppi, Baldassare (1706–85) Venetian composer, of numerous serious and comic operas, as well as toccatas. No. 3 may have been an insert aria for his *The Marriage of Dorina*.

Gerl, Franz Xaver (1764–1827) Austrian bass. A member of Schickaneder's company from 1787 to 1792, he sang Osmin, Figaro, Don Giovanni and Sarastro. No. 24 was written for him to sing at a concert at Schickaneder's theatre, with the double-bass virtuoso Friedrich Pischelberger.

German Dance Term for the triple-time dance which gave rise to the waltz and the ländler. Mozart's set K. 571 was written for the Redoutensaal and dated 21 February 1789 in his catalogue.

Gigue Quick compound-time dance. Mozart composed K. 574, modelled on Handel, into the notebook of the Leipzig court organist on 16 May 1789; he was on his way to Berlin with Prince Karl Lichnowsky.

Goldoni, Carlo (1707–93) Venetian playwright and librettist. His more than fifty opera buffa librettos include *La finta semplice*, of which Mozart set a version in 1764, and *The Marriage* (or *The Marriage of Dorina*), first set by Galuppi. No. 3 may have been written as an insert aria for this piece. *The Good-Hearted Grouch* was based on a Goldoni play.

Good-Hearted Grouch, The *(Il burbero di buon core)* Opera by Martín y Soler to a libretto by da Ponte. Mozart wrote two arias for Louise Villeneuve to sing as Lucilla in the revival given on 9 November 1789. 'Chi sà qual sia' (No. 4) was to be sung in the first act, at the point where Lucilla's husband Giocondo has, without explanation, forbidden her to interfere in his family affairs, and left her perplexed and alone. 'Vado, ma dove?' (No. 19) belongs to the second act. Giocondo's business has collapsed, and Lucilla has been made to feel that she is responsible.

Indiscreet Inquirer, The *(Il curioso indiscreto)* Opera by
Anfossi to a libretto possibly by Bertati, after Cervantes.
Mozart wrote three arias for the production of this opera in
Vienna on 30 June 1783: two for Aloysia Lange and one for
Valentin Adamberger, all to new, anonymous texts. 'Vorrei
spiegarvi' (No. 25) was placed early in the first act. The
Marchese Calandrano, wanting to prove the virtue of his
intended bride Clorinda, has persuaded his friend the Count
of Ripaverde to pay court to her. A first attempt failed, but
at a second she began to weaken: now she relinquishes the
Count and bids him return to his beloved Emilia (the refer-
ences to these other characters are avoided in *The Jewel Box*).
'Per pietà' (No. 17) belongs near the start of the second act.
The Count has overheard a conversation between Clorinda
and Aurelio, another friend of the Marchese; he is cut with
jealousy. After the aria he accuses Clorinda to the Marchese.
She overhears this conversation and is enraged. He is persuaded of her innocence and begs forgiveness: her reaction
is 'No, che non sei capace' (No. 18).

Lange, Aloysia *(c.* 1760–1839) German soprano. Mozart fell
in love with her while he was staying in Mannheim during
the winter of 1777–8. In 1778 he wrote three arias for her,
including the one that became on revision No. 5. Two years
later she married the actor and painter Joseph Lange (her
maiden name had been Weber), and two years after that
Mozart married her younger sister Constanze. From 1779 to
1792 she sang regularly in Vienna, and Mozart continued to
write music for her: No. 27 for her to sing at a benefit concert
in 1782, the next year another concert aria as well as the
two arias for *The Indiscreet Inquirer*, and in 1786 the part
of Mme Herz in *The Impresario*. All this music together
provides a remarkable portrait – Mozart's most comprehen-
sive vocal likeness – of what was clearly a remarkable voice.
She was also Donna Anna in the Vienna *Don Giovanni*, and
is recorded as having sung No. 18 several times in concert.

Lucky Jealous Women, The *(Le gelosie fortunate)* Opera by

Anfossi to a libretto by Livigni. Mozart's insert aria, with an elaborated text possibly by da Ponte, is delivered by Monsieur Girò as a lesson to Don Pompeo in the ways of women. The Vienna production of this opera, given on 2 June 1788, included music by nine composers.

Mandini, Stefano (1750–?c. 1810) Italian singer. He sang in Vienna from 1783 to 1788, creating the role of the Count, with his wife Maria as Marcellina; he was also Pippo in *The Village Girl Ravished.*

Marriage of Dorina, The *(Le nozze di Dorina)* Opera by Galuppi to a libretto by Goldoni. Mozart's insert aria, dated 26 October 1775, was possibly written for a production in Salzburg, but if so the action must have been altered, since in the original the maidservant Dorina sings teasingly to two suitors, whereas here she addresses only one. The text Mozart set diverges from Goldoni after two words; the text in *The Jewel Box* after one.

Martín y Soler, Vicente (1754–1806) Spanish composer. He wrote operas for Madrid and then for Italian theatres in 1779–85. In 1785 he moved to Vienna, and began the collaboration with da Ponte that produced *The Good-Hearted Grouch* (1786), *An Odd Thing* (1786) and *The Tree of Diana* (1787), of which the two last were much more popular than Mozart's operas: Mozart duly quoted from *An Odd Thing* in Don Giovanni's supper music. By the end of 1788 Martín y Soler had moved to St Petersburg, and so was not present to supervise the Vienna revival of *The Good-Hearted Grouch* for which Mozart wrote two insert arias.

Metastasio, Pietro (1698–1782) Roman poet. He was the dominant opera seria librettist from the late 1720s onwards, and from 1730 lived in Vienna as court poet. Mozart set adaptations of his *Bethulia Liberated* in 1771, *Scipio's Dream* in 1772, *The Shepherd King* in 1775 and *The Clemency of Titus* in 1791, and often extracted texts from other librettos for concert arias. The sources for the Italian words of

Nos. 5, 9, 14 and 20 were, respectively, his *The Chinese Hero*, *Olympia*, *Themistocles* and *Dido Abandoned*.

Mozart, Wolfgang Amadeus (1756–91) Composer.

Olympia *(Olimpiade)* Libretto by Metastasio. Mozart took from it the words for No. 9, composed for Ludwig Fischer and dated 19 March 1787. King Clistene is thrown into turmoil at the appearance of a man who made an attempt on his life, not knowing that this is his son.

Palmini, Antonio Italian tenor, named on the autograph as the intended singer of No. 10.

Palomba, Giuseppe *(fl.* 1769–1825) Italian librettist. He is credited with more than three hundred librettos: eleven or twelve of them were comedies for Cimarosa, including *The Two Barons of Rocca Azzurra*. In this case, rather unusually, Mozart followed the original libretto in his insert aria.

Pantalone The fall guy of the commedia dell'arte: the type of the deceived father, the deluded husband.

Pedrolino The ancestor of Pierrot in the commedia dell'arte.

Petrosellini, Giuseppe (1727–*c.* 1799) Italian librettist. He is credited with two opera buffa librettos Mozart set, or began to set, before his collaboration with da Ponte: *La finta giardiniera* and *The Deluded Husband*. His other librettos included *The Abstracted Man*, though here Mozart's insert arias use texts not in the original.

Piccinni, Niccolò (1728–1800) Italian composer. His prodigious output of comic and serious operas – generally composed for Italian theatres, though he also had periods in Paris – included *The Abstracted Man*, for which Mozart wrote insert arias.

Ponte, Lorenzo da (1749–1838) Italian librettist. He lived in Vienna from 1781 to 1792, and afterwards in London and New York. He was, of course, most famously the librettist of *Figaro*, *Don Giovanni* and *Così fan tutte* (and thereby also of No. 15), but he may have provided Mozart with words too for the arias made for *The Lucky Jealous Women* and

The Good-Hearted Grouch, the latter being a libretto of his own.

Storace, Nancy (1765–1817) English soprano. She sang in Vienna between 1783 and 1787, and was the intended Eugenia in *The Deluded Husband*. Mozart also wrote the part of Susanna for her, and the concert aria 'Ch'io mi scordi di te'.

Themistocles *(Temistocle)* Libretto by Metastasio. It is the source of the original text for No. 14, which may have been written as a concert piece or for insertion in an operatic setting. Sebaste's political ambitions have been betrayed by Princess Roxane: he gives vent to his feelings.

Two Barons of Rocca Azzurra, The *(I due baroni di Rocca Azzurra)* Opera by Cimarosa to a libretto by Palomba. Mozart's insert aria was written for a Vienna performance on 6 September 1789. The younger of the two barons is expecting the arrival of his new bride Madama Laura, but Franchetto tries to substitute his sister Sandra in the role. Laura sings the aria late in the first act, at the end of an altercation with Sandra.

Varesco, Giambattista *(c.* 1736–1805) The court chaplain in Salzburg from 1766, and librettist of *Idomeneo* and *The Cairo Goose*.

Village Girl Ravished, The *(La villanella rapita)* Opera by Bianchi to a libretto by Bertati. Mozart wrote two ensembles, with new words, for the Vienna performance on 28 November 1785; the singers were Coltellini, Calvesi, Mandini and Bussani. 'Mandina amabile' (No. 8) comes near the end of the first act, and was the only vocal composition of Mozart's to be published in full score during his lifetime. Mandina, the simple girl of the title, is being seduced by the Count, but the scene is interrupted by her swain Pippo. By means of a sleeping draught the Count then has Mandina taken to his castle, where she is discovered in the quartet. 'Dite almeno' (No. 12) by Pippo and her father Biagio. The tumult brings the Count onto the scene, to threaten to dispatch these peasants.

Villeneuve, Louise She joined the opera company in Vienna in 1789, and within a year had received from Mozart insert arias for *The Two Barons of Rocca Azzurra* and *The Good-Hearted Grouch*, as well as the part of Dorabella.

Wendling, Dorothea (1736–1811) German soprano. Mozart became acquainted with the Wendlings, as with the Webers, when he was in Mannheim in 1777–8. He wrote No. 20 for her; she and her sister-in-law Elisabeth Wendling then created the roles of Ilia and Elettra.

Paul Griffiths